# Compiler Construction

## *Explore Parser Generation and Abstract Syntax Trees*

# Table of Contents

# Chapter 1. Introduction

Welcome to this Special Report, tailored meticulously to transform the intricate subject of Compiler Construction into an engaging and enlightening experience. Our report is dedicated to delving deep into the profoundly important, yet often overlooked realms of Parser Generation and Abstract Syntax Trees. Despite the technical nature of the subject, we promise a journey through these complex domains, making them as down-to-earth, relatable, and intriguing as we can. From understanding the nature of parsers and their generation, to unraveling the mystical layers of Abstract Syntax Trees - this report is aimed to unveil the magic behind the functioning of the compilers we use daily. Carry with you your curiosity, and we promise to escort you into the fascinating world of Compiler Construction. Don't miss this chance to acquire a rare insight into a science that is seamlessly integrated into our tech-reliant lives. So, buckle up and let the exploration begin!

# Chapter 2. Introducing Compiler Construction: A Primer

Compilers are among the most complex programs written, and understanding their construction can seem daunting. However, breaking down the process into simple stages can render the task manageable and exciting. In this primer, we shall provide a dive deep into the fundamentals.

## 2.1. What are Compilers?

Compilers are essentially translators - robust tools that convert high-level source code, written in languages like Python, Java, or C++, into machine code, an extremely low-level language that a computer can understand and execute. The primary intention of building a compiler is to automate the process of code transformation, optimizing the final output to achieve maximum efficiency.

The process of compilation can be analogized with the translation of a novel from one language to another. The story (source code) stays the same, but the language (syntax and semantics) changes. The translator (compiler) must be proficient in both languages and must understand the storytelling conventions (execution paradigms) in both contexts to generate a fluent, coherent translation (working program).

## 2.2. Phases of Compiler

The end-to-end journey of source code through a compiler is fragmented into several stages, namely – lexical analysis, syntax analysis, semantic analysis, intermediate code generation, code optimization, and code generation. Each phase handles a particular aspect of the translation process, working synergistically to transform source code to machine code.

1. **Lexical Analysis**: In this commencement phase, the compiler breaks down the source code into basic elements known as tokens. These tokens represent atomic elements of the language like keywords, identifiers, literals, and more.

2. **Syntax Analysis**: The syntax analyzer or parser validates the grammatical structure of the code by organizing tokens derived from lexical analysis into a syntax tree based on the grammar rules of the language.

3. **Semantic Analysis**: This rigorous phase is concerned with enforcing language-specific rules, variable declarations, and scope, and type rules, ensuring that the logical structure of the code is correct.

4. **Intermediate Code Generation**: The compiler generates platform-independent intermediate code from the verified syntax tree which can be easily transformed into the target machine code.

5. **Code Optimization**: This influential phase focuses on improving the intermediate code for better performance in terms of execution time and space efficiency.

6. **Code Generation**: Transforms optimized intermediate code into the final machine code.

# 2.3. Structure of Compilers

Compilers are typically organized into a sequence of modules, each of which is responsible for one phase of the compilation process. This modular structure provides several benefits in terms of debugging, maintenance, and manageability. In a broad sense, the compilation process is divided into two primary parts: the analysis part and the synthesis part.

1. **Analysis Part**: This segment, often referred to as the `front-end` of a compiler, focuses on checking if the program's syntax is correct. It also ascertains the correct semantics and transforms the source program into an intermediate representation. The lexical analyzer, syntax analyzer, and semantic analyzer - they all reside in this block.

2. **Synthesis Part**: This section, the `back-end` of the compiler, is responsible for the code generation phase from the intermediate representation. It optimizes the translated code for efficient execution.

## 2.4. Why Compiler Construction Matters?

In today's digital era, compilers play an indomitable role. They're the unsung heroes behind any software's functioning, acting as influential building blocks of modern computing. Here are several key reasons why understanding compiler construction matters:

1. To write efficient code: When you know how the compiler works, you can write code that can be compiled more efficiently, minimizing run-time overheads.

2. For language development: Whether you're aiming to design a new language or extend an existing one, knowledge of compiler construction is indispensable to create an efficient compiler for the new language.

3. Debugger tools: Developers who understand the working of a compiler are in a better position to build robust debugging tools and interpret the output of existing tools.

4. Job interviews: Questions about compilers, especially optimization done by compilers, frequently appear in technical

interviews for software engineering roles.

Compiler construction is an intricate yet exhilarating journey that provides a complete understanding of high-level to machine-level code conversion. Although it's complex, if unfolded properly, you can see the layers of logic and algorithms that are seamlessly bridged to produce efficient machine code from human-readable programming languages. So, let's keep exploring this fascinating realm, full of puzzles and challenges. The more we uncover, the closer we get to realizing the full potential of computers.

In the following chapters, we will embark further on this exploration, starting with the nature of parsers and their generation, which forms the backbone of the syntax analysis phase. As we advance, we will delve into the formation of Abstract Syntax Trees - a step that plays a crucial role in the semantic analysis phase. We promise to unravel the magic of compilers bit by bit in the subsequent sections. Stay tuned, as this will be an engaging expedition into the very foundations that have shaped modern computing.

# Chapter 3. Breaking Down Languages: Lexer and Lexical Analysis

In the grand scheme of compiler construction, understanding languages is a fundamental step. It forms the cornerstone of all compiler activities, transmuting human-readable code into machine-understandable instructions. Lexical analysis, operated by the lexer or lexical analyzer, is the first phase of this transformation.

## 3.1. Let's Understand Lexical Analysis

Lexical Analysis is the process of converting a sequence of characters (input to the compiler) into a sequence of 'tokens'. A token is a symbolic representation of a set of characters having collective meaning. It's the basic atomic unit of programming languages, akin to atoms in the universe – they're the smallest distinguishable unit.

Example tokens include keywords (like 'if', 'else', 'function'), identifiers (variable names), operators (+, -, *, /), delimiters (',', ';'), and literals ('4', 'true', etc.).

## 3.2. Lexer: The Craft behind Token Generation

The Lexer, or Lexical Analyzer, performs the role of the sender in the communication model of a compiler. It reads the source program's character streams, groups them into lexemes, and produces the corresponding tokens.

Its primary responsibility is to simplify the task for the parser. By grouping characters into atomic units (tokens), it reduces the complexity and computational overhead of the parser. So instead of the parser having to comprehend each character, byte by byte, it interprets the tokens - an easier and more efficient approach.

## 3.3. The Details of the Lexer Process

Let's break down the working of the lexer into smaller steps for a clear understanding:

1. **Reading Input Streams:** The lexer reads input (source code) as a stream of characters.

2. **Breaking Into Lexemes:** It then breaks this stream down into meaningful sequences referred to as lexemes.

3. **Generating Tokens:** Post this, it maps these lexemes into specified tokens.

4. **Producing Token Streams:** Lastly, it conjures a stream of these tokens to pass onto the parser.

In case of an invalid token, where the lexer can't recognize the incoming sequence of characters, it flags an error. This typically happens when we violate the rules of a language's syntax.

## 3.4. Challenges in Lexical Analysis

Creating a robust lexer might seem straightforward but it presents its own challenges. For one, the lexer should effectively manage white spaces and comments as part of pre-processing. Handling these correctly ensures that insignificant elements in syntax and semantics don't confuse the compiler or the parser.

Moreover, the lexical analyzer must adeptly tackle ambiguous constructs such as 'a = b * -c'. Here, is '-c' an unary operator on variable 'c', or is it a new variable '-c'? The lexical analyzer must decide and generate tokens that ensure the correct parsing downstream.

## 3.5. Concluding the Process

To sum up, Lexical Analysis marks the beginning of the compiler's symphony. It reads source code, identifies lexemes, and generates tokens. The lexer is the driving force behind this process—a pre-processing tool that takes raw, unformatted text and converts it into meaningful tokens, ensuring what follows is more efficient and accurate.

In our quest of deciphering compiler construction, understanding the concept of lexical analysis and the role of a lexical analyzer acts as a significant stepping stone. Further down the line, these tokens become the bedrock upon which we construct syntax trees, directly influencing how compilers interpret and execute code.

This in-depth understanding of Lexer and Lexical Analysis allows one sight into the first layer of the compiler's magical world, setting the stage for the next phase - Syntax Analysis, where we introduce you to parsers and their generation. Through a seamless, enlightening process, we will continue unearthing the mysteries of compiler construction. And remember, as in any journey, each step counts; so let's march on, token by token, into the deeper layers of compiler design.

# Chapter 4. The Art of Parsing: An Overview

Every voyage begins with a single step, and ours starts from understanding that core aspect of compiler construction - Parsing. We'll set off on this fascinating exploration while making it as graspable, relatable, and intriguing as we can. Without further ado, let's plunge straight in.

Parsing, at its essence, is the process of dissecting and interpreting a sequence of tokens with the aim of understanding the actual 'meaning' or structure it portrays. This 'meaning' or structure is an essence in computer science, particularly in compiler construction, where it aids in translating high-level code into machine-friendly instructions.

## 4.1. Understanding The Notion of Parsers

The first stepping stone on our path to comprehend parsing in compiler construction is understanding what a parser is. In the simplest terms, a parser is a component of the compiler that functions to interpret the combination of tokens passed onto it by the lexical analyzer (also known as the lexer), another vital cog in the compiler. The parser constructs a parse tree, a symbolic representation of the input. This parse tree follows certain rules dictated by a formal grammar, such as a context-free grammar that provides the underlying structure for constructing the sentences of the language.

Creating a parser, however, is no easy task - it's equivalent to developing a bridge that navigates from high-level language syntax to symbolic representation, a bridge that must endure all kinds of inputs it receives. This, indeed, is the true art of parsing - crafting a translator that remains robust against valid variations while rejecting erroneous ones.

Let's look more closely into the two broad categories of parsers; top-down and bottom-up parsers.

## 4.2. Top-Down Parsers

Top-down parsers, as the name implies, commence their parsing task from the root of the parse tree and follow the path down to the leaves. This category of parsers evaluates the start symbol and begins to anticipate what the input would be, pertaining to the rules of the language's grammar.

Among the top-down parsers, a variant known as recursive descent parsers stands out due to its simplicity. These parsers manifest themselves as a set of recursive procedures where each procedure directly translates a grammar rule. However, note that non-recursive parsers also exist within the top-down category and are notably useful where recursion may result in considerable resource usage.

Despite the relative simplicity of implementation, top-down parsers come with their own limitations. One notable roadblock is the difficulty they face while trying to handle left-recursive grammar rules, which may result in the parser entering an infinite loop. Moreover, top-down parsers find it challenging to deal with ambiguous grammars.

## 4.3. Bottom-Up Parsers

Unlike their top-down counterparts, bottom-up parsers embark on their journey from leaves (tokens) and ascend up to the root of the tree. Rather than predicting the input, these parsers continue to read in the input until a target can be inferred in retrospect. This particular strength makes bottom-up parsers potent in handling more complex grammatical structures, including left recursion.

Among the bottom-up parsers, LR parsers (Left-to-right scans of the input, Rightmost derivation) are pivotal and are popular for their capacity to handle a broad range of grammars. They require careful crafting, and the process can be quite involved, but the potential payoff is huge.

Each parser has its own unique strengths and weaknesses. Therefore, when constructing a compiler, it's crucial to select the category of parser that best aligns with the particular language's grammar requirements.

# 4.4. Parser Generators

With the abundance of variety in high-level languages, creating a customized parser for each language is a hefty task. Therefore, tools called parser generators are commonly used. Parser generators take a formal grammar of a language as an input and generate a parser as the output. They are the unsung heroes behind the scenes making compiler construction more manageable.

The use of parser generators not only eases the task of compiler construction but also maintains the quality and uniformity of the parsers. There are numerous different parser generators available that cater to various needs, from ANTLR and Bison to JavaCC and Yacc. Each of these has its own unique attributes and features.

# 4.5. The role of Grammar

The journey from human-like high-level language to a structure that a machine can digest is guided and governed by the grammar rules of the language. Every language is endowed with a formal grammar that dictates the sentence structure for that language. It's the lighthouse beaming towards the parser, channeling it on how to shape the parse tree.

Grammar lays the bedrock foundation, enabling the parser to analyse whether a piece of code adheres to the syntactic rules of the language. Consequently, it navigates the parser towards the correct construction of the parse tree.

In compiler construction, the commonly used formal grammar is the context-free grammar (CFG). CFG is a type of formal grammar where every production rule is of the form $V \rightarrow w$, where $V$ is a single nonterminal symbol, and $w$ is a string of terminals and/or nonterminals.

Understanding formal grammar is an essential instrument in our toolkit as we explore further into the magic behind compiler construction.

# 4.6. Wrapping up

So here we are - we have sailed across the fundamental concepts of parsing; from the essence of parsers, the contrasts between top-down and bottom-up parsing, the convenience of parser generators, and the role of grammar has in steering the ship. These concepts create the foundational knowledge we'll need as we explore further into the magic behind compiler construction.

The next chapter will unveil another pivotal component of compiler construction - Abstract Syntax Trees. Hold onto the curiosity and the insights you've drawn from this chapter as we continue our voyage into the fascinating world of compiler construction.

# Chapter 5. Understanding Parser Generation: Techniques and Tools

In the heart of compiler construction lies parser generation, a crucial step that aids in the transformation of high-level code into an intermediate representation. This journey aims to become your guidebook to an in-depth understanding of parser generation, its diverse techniques, and the tools employed.

## 5.1. Structure of a Parser

A parser qualifies as the core component of a compiler. Its main function is to check whether the input tokens, typically from a lexer, conform to the syntactic rules of the language in question. These syntactic rules are typically defined by the language's grammar. Furthermore, the parser constructs a parse or syntax tree, which serves as a bridge between the source code and the target code.

A parser comprises two primary stages: the Lexical Analyzer (or Lexer) and the Syntax Analyzer. The Lexer takes in the source code and breaks it down into a stream of tokens. These tokens are identifiable language components, such as identifiers, operators, punctuation, etc. The Syntax Analyzer then takes this stream of tokens as input and, based on the defined grammar of the programming language, constructs a parse or syntax tree.

## 5.2. Parser Generation Techniques

There exist a number of techniques to go about parser generation. Our focus lies primarily on two: Top-down parsing and Bottom-up parsing.

### 5.2.1. Top-Down Parsing

Top-Down parsing, as the name suggests, starts from the top, or the initial symbol, and tries to derive the input stream from it. The primary class of top-down parsers is Recursive Descent Parsers, which attempt to match the input with the right-hand side of grammar rules, coming back (recursing) if the match is unsuccessful.

The second class of top-down parsers is Predictive Parsers. This is a non-recursive parsing method that, instead of backtracking, predicts which of the productions to use based on the next few input symbols. Predictive Parsers require the grammar to be left-factored and non-left recursive.

### 5.2.2. Bottom-Up Parsing

Bottom-up parsing starts from the input stream and attempts to reach the initial symbol. The predominant class here is Shift-Reduce Parsers, which operate by shifting inputs onto a stack until they can be reduced to a grammar rule.

One main subcategory of Shift-Reduce Parsers is the LR parsers (Left-to-right, Rightmost derivation), which can handle a larger set of grammars than top-down parsers. However, they can be more complex to set up. Furthermore, LR parsers have several subclasses, including SLR, LALR, and Canonical LR parsers. The LR parsing method is often preferred for its completeness and its efficient use of stack space.

# 5.3. Parser Generation Tools

Several parser generator tools aid in the construction of parsers. A few notable ones include:

- ANTLR: ANother Tool for Language Recognition, more commonly known as ANTLR, is a powerful tool for constructing recognizers, interpreters, compilers, and translators from grammatical descriptions comprising of lexer, parser, and tree rules.

- Bison: It is a general-purpose parser generator that converts a grammar description into a C, C++, or Java program to parse that grammar. Bison is an extension of the original Yacc (Yet Another Compiler Compiler).

- Flex: Primarily a Lexical Analyzer tool, it is often used in conjunction with Bison in parser creation. It can generate analyzers in either C or C++.

- JavaCC: Java Compiler Compiler, JavaCC, is the most popular parser generator for use with Java applications. JavaCC facilitates designing a parser from scratch with its simple and practical syntax and its application to both lexical and syntactic analyses.

# 5.4. Concluding Thoughts

Understanding parser generation forms the backbone of appreciating the complexities of compiler construction. It grants an all-encompassing perspective on how high-level language is calibrated into machine-understandable directions. Our perception of parsed code aids in the seamless flow of this transition, transforming an intimidating task into a manageable series of small steps. After all, big things are but small things brought together, and compiler construction is no exception.

Though complex, the subject of parsing science can be fascinating. With curiosity as the compass, continued exploration can lead to profound computer science and engineering insights, greatly benefiting anyone seeking to comprehend the wizardry that runs behind the scenes in our everyday tech-dependent lives.

Perhaps now when you glimpse at your code, you'll notice the legwork the parser does in the back-end to ensure a succinctly executed command, and in the process, appreciate the invisible magic of compiler construction. The journey to understanding parser generation might have been lengthy, but the destination makes it rewarding.

# Chapter 6. Top-Down vs. Bottom-Up Parsing: A Comparative Analysis

In the domain of compiler construction, parsing plays a significant role, serving as a bridge linking the human-readable source code to a computer-understandable form. Developers around the globe have adopted two main strategies for parsing: Top-Down Parsing and Bottom-Up Parsing. In this segment, we will draw a line of comparison between these two parsing technique giants based on various parameters including complexity, efficiency, applicability, among others.

## 6.1. Understanding Parsing

Parsing is the process of analyzing a sequence of tokens (usually the output of lexical analysis) based on a specified grammar. In essence, it's the task of identifying a structure within a stream of tokens that we can map onto the rules of a formal language.

Once the source code of a program is transformed into a sequence of tokens via a lexer, the parser takes over the task of creating a parse tree from these tokens. The parse tree is an essential part of "syntax analysis", the second phase in the process of compiler construction.

## 6.2. Top-Down Parsing

Top-Down parsing starts from the root or the start symbol and works its way down to the leaves of the parse tree. The aim is to construct a parse tree for an input string beginning from the start symbol and continually replacing one of the non-terminals in the current string by one of its production rules.

Non-terminal symbols denote constructs of a language that can be broken down into smaller constructs, while terminal symbols relate to the lowest level constructs, often individual characters or lexemes.

Top-Down parsing can further be classified into:

- Recursive Descent Parsing

- Predictive Parsing

The main attraction of top-down parsing methods is their conceptual simplicity, but they may also fall into the pitfall of infinite recursion for left-recursive grammar.

# 6.3. Bottom-Up Parsing

Bottom-Up parsing can be thought of as the opposite of Top-Down parsing. It starts from the bottom i.e., the leaves (the set of possible inputs), and works its way up towards the root of the parse tree i.e., the start symbol.

The goal of bottom-up parsing is to find a right-hand side of some production that matches the input string, replace it with the left-hand side (non-terminal), and continue this process until we manage to reduce the entire string to the start symbol alone.

Bottom-Up parsing can further be classified into:

- Operator-Precedence Parsing

- Shift-Reduce Parsing

- LR Parsing

The main appeal of bottom-up parsing is its ability to handle a more extensive range of grammar compared to top-down parsing.

# 6.4. Comparing Top-Down and Bottom-Up Parsing

Let's now dive into an in-depth comparison between top-down and bottom-up parsing algorithms.

**Simultaneous Processing:** Top-down parsers start from the input and the grammar's start symbol simultaneously and match them throughout the execution while bottom-up parsers first process the input, storing it until they match the grammar.

**Types of Grammar Handled:** Bottom-up parsers are capable of parsing most general types of grammars, including left-recursive grammars, which can pose a significant problem to top-down parsers.

**Detection of Syntactic Errors:** Top-down parsers can detect syntactic errors (i.e., errors violating the syntax rules of the programming language) as soon as they are encountered in the input. Conversely, bottom-up parsers often don't detect errors until the end of the input, making them slightly less efficient in error detection and recovery.

**Parse Tree Generation:** While top-down parsers create the parse tree from the root to the leaves, bottom-up parsers generate the parse tree from the leaves to the root.

**Implementation Complexity:** It is generally easier to implement top-down parsing, especially recursive descent, in code compared to bottom-up parsing, which makes use of more complex methods such as Constructing LR Parsing Tables.

**Efficiency:** A factor where top-down parsers shine is efficiency, by virtue of their speed. Bottom-up parsers are slower due to the vast number of states kept in memory.

# 6.5. A Final Word

As we have seen, the choice between top-down and bottom-up parsing largely depends on the specifics of the task at hand: the complexity of your grammar, your available resources, and your tolerance for errors and extensibility. Make an informed decision by considering these aspects and understanding the trade-offs involved in choosing either path, as both come with their own strength and weaknesses. Remember, the choice ultimately lies in striking the right balance between performance, error detection, and complexity.

The beauty of compiler construction is the blend of theory and practice, art and science. As you delve deeper into the domain, the stories behind every algorithm or tool unfold, leading to your journey of understanding and, eventually, mastery.

# Chapter 7. Unveiling Abstract Syntax Trees: Nature and Importance

Unearthing the concept of Abstract Syntax Trees (ASTs) calls for a return to the fundamentals of compiler design, which is a complicated balance between efficiency and accuracy in translating high-level programming languages into machine code. An essential role of the compiler is to parse the source code, verifying its syntax according to pre-determined grammar rules and to represent the program's structure logically. This logical representation is the AST, an abstract and simplified visualization of the program's underlying structure.

## 7.1. The Nature of Abstract Syntax Trees

Abstract Syntax Trees are a fundamental aspect of the parsing process in a compiler and form the main pathway from source code to machine code. ASTs represent the syntactical structure of programs through hierarchical tree-like structures. In essence, an AST is like a skeleton of a program, stripping away unnecessary details like parentheses, semicolons, and braces, focusing instead on expressing the nesting structure and the operations performed.

At the heart of an AST are nodes, with each node in the tree symbolizing a construct occurring in the source code. The root of the tree usually represents the entire program, while the leaf nodes represent the lowest level constructs like variables or constants. Non-leaf nodes, on the other hand, denote higher-level constructs such as operations or expressions.

# 7.2. The Need for Abstract Syntax Trees

The question arises - why do we need an Abstract Syntax Tree? Once source code undergoes lexical analysis, where it is broken down into tokens, why not convert these tokens directly into machine language? The answer is twofold:

1. **Validation of Syntax**: Directly converting tokens to machine language ignores the formation of valid statements or expressions. The AST helps to ensure the correctness of the source program's syntax following grammar rules. Any invalid syntax would not be converted into a correct AST, signaling an error to the compiler.

2. **Understanding Program Structure**: ASTs capture the hierarchical structure of the source program and allow the compiler to understand the logical flow of the program. This clarity allows for the implementation of program transformations and refactorings, which are crucial aspects of code optimization.

# 7.3. Deriving ASTs: The Process

Deriving an Abstract Syntax Tree from source code involves the compilation step of syntactic analysis or parsing. The input for this process is the series of tokens produced by the lexical analysis phase. The parser then constructs the AST by applying grammar rules defined for the source language. If these grammar rules are not met, the parser signals a syntax error.

Upon the successful construction of the AST, the semantics of the source code become clear. Each tree node represents an operation and the links to the subtrees (children nodes) denote the operands. For example, for a mathematical operation like addition, the " operator would be a node, and the numbers being added would be the subtrees linked to the ". Running depth-first traversal of the AST would provide the order of operation execution.

# 7.4. The Vitality of ASTs in Compiler Optimization

One of the major mandates of any compiler is to enhance the performance of the subsequent executable code. The AST is a critical tool in this endeavor.

Post constructing the AST and while it's in memory, the compiler could perform optimizations like constant folding, dead code elimination, or loop invariant code motion. To illustrate, consider constant folding. If the code includes arithmetic operations on constants, such as '5+3', it can be replaced with '8' during compile-time, thereby reducing computation during execution. These are called 'local optimizations' as they involve a single AST node and its immediate children.

There are also 'global optimizations' that involve reordering of instructions or eliminating common subexpressions. These require a broader view of the code and may involve several AST nodes. For example, if two different parts of the code include the same costly computation, it could be computed once, stored, and then reused. Reducing unnecessary computations enhances the efficiency of the resulting program.

# Chapter 8. Harnessing ASTs beyond Compilers

While ASTs primarily facilitate compiler functioning, their use isn't restricted to compilers. With the rising need for tooling in the software development lifecycle, ASTs help enable better development tools. For instance, Integrated Development Environments (IDEs) leverage ASTs to provide syntax highlighting, code suggestions, and auto-completion. Furthermore, static code analyzers use ASTs to identify potential bugs, code smells, or security vulnerabilities without executing the program.

## 8.1. Abstract Syntax Trees: An Essential, Not A Luxury

Understanding and appreciating the concept of Abstract Syntax Trees is fundamental to grasping the intricacies of compiler construction. These trees not only empower compilers to translate source code accurately and efficiently but also enhance code quality and readability. With tooling and optimization capabilities, these simple tree structures play a crucial role in the landscape of modern programming environments.

The AST, though abstract, bears significant concrete impacts on the run-time efficiency and development lifecycle of software programs. Its potential beyond compilers showcases its versatility. As our journey in compiler construction continues, it is evident that such abstract concepts offer an insightful behind-the-scenes glimpse into the making and running of the software world as we know it. So, as we contemplate the humble Abstract Syntax Tree today, let's appreciate its artistry and utility in shaping the digital realities of tomorrow.

# Chapter 9. Generating Abstract Syntax Trees: From Theory to Practice

Console commands, iconic black screens, the cozy embrace of an Integrated Development Environment (IDE), all have one common fulcrum - compilers. No matter the programming language we speak, compilers impeccably translate and execute our coded conversations. An essential, yet not often comprehended mechanism operating behind these translations is the construction of Abstract Syntax Trees (ASTs).

## 9.1. The Essence of Abstract Syntax Trees

ASTs are an integral part of any compiler's operation. These rooted trees are the visual embodiment of the language grammar and represent the structure of a code segment without any frills. Each node represents a construct in the code, with the tree's hierarchy denoting the execution sequence. Language elements such as expressions, conditions, loops, and function calls are the shared occupants of the AST nodes. The beauty of ASTs lies in their simplicity and generality - allowing us to study and manipulate code structure sans syntactic noise.

## 9.2. Unleashing the Parser: The First Step

Construction of ASTs starts with parsing. A parser takes a string of tokens (output from the lexing phase) and confirms that they can form a valid sentence as per the language grammar. These tokens are combined according to syntax rules to build ASTs. In our journey ahead, our guiding stars will be Context Free Grammars (CFGs), which lay down the syntax rules for most programming languages.

# 9.3. Context Free Grammars (CFGs)

CFGs are grammar systems used to parse a sentence (code), wherein the rules are termed as productions. Each production sees the replacement of a non-terminal symbol with a collection of terminal or non-terminal symbols. A non-terminal symbol is a syntax category, such as an expression or a statement. Terminal symbols are the end characters themselves - like the numbers or arithmetic operators.

CFGs help translate the structural relationships of symbols occurring in the language. Parsing utilizes these CFGs to check the validity of this sequence of symbols and then use the same for construction of the AST.

# 9.4. Recursive Descent Parsing

One standard method for generation of ASTs is Recursive Descent Parsing. This approach corresponds to a top-down parser that starts its journey from the 'root' (initiating syntax rule). It uses one procedure for every non-terminal symbol of a CFG.

The key is its 'recursive' nature. To handle a non-terminal symbol from any procedure, it instantiates the procedure associated with that symbol. The order and number of procedure invocations reflect the tree structure. The recursion ends when terminal symbols are encountered, and the path leads back to the root, building an AST on the way.

As straightforward as this approach might appear, it has its pitfalls. It is unable to handle left-recursive rules and finite repetition of symbols. For such circumstances, we turn to another parser – the

Parser Generator.

# 9.5. Parser Generators - The Triumph Over Finite Repetitions

Parser Generators can automate the construction of parsers, which follow a broader specification of CFGs. They embrace finite repetitions & left-recursive rules, overshadowing the limitations of Recursive Descent Parsing. This leads to the generation of LR parsers - a class of bottom-up parsers that can handle a larger set of CFGs.

Let's simplify the concept with an example. Recall the rule to construct 'n' number of statements (`stmts → stmt stmts | ▯`). For n = 3, with Recursive Descent Parsing, you would need 3 productions! Instead, the parser generator simplifies it with the form `stmts → stmt*`.

With these enhanced capabilities, Parser Generators become the predominant choice for generating ASTs in modern compiler structures.

# 9.6. Designing an Abstract Syntax Tree

Having dipped our toes into parser generation, let's turn our attention to designing ASTs. An AST requires the representation of each programming construct as a distinguished node. For instance, 'for loop' and 'condition statements' are depicted by separate nodes.

Designing them requires an astute understanding of both your language and the way it's structured, as each language element is associated with a specific node in the AST.

For instance, a binary operation like addition will be represented with a node "add" having two children representing the operands. ASTs disregard the less-relevant components (like parenthesis and semicolons in C++), creating a leaner, cleaner tree structure for easier manipulation.

# 9.7. From Parse Trees to Abstract Syntax Trees

It's noteworthy that initially, a parser doesn't directly create an AST but forms a parse tree instead. The parse tree is a more comprehensive representation encompassing everything from the source code, unlike an AST that omits details and focuses only on relevant information.

Transforming a parse tree into an AST involves pruning non-essential elements (intermediate nodes with a single child, nodes representing commas, semicolons, etc.). The resulting AST is compact, devoid of clutter, and paints a succinct picture of the code structure.

# 9.8. Practical Aspects

After appreciating the theory of ASTs, it's time to examine their practical construction. ASTs are typically constructed in memory via objects. Each node in an AST is portrayed as an object of a class representing the construct. A node includes details about its type and the relations it shares with other nodes.

For instance, take an 'addition operation' in C++. It might be represented as an object of the 'AddExpression' class, containing pointers to objects that represent operands. Object-oriented programming principles are extensively leveraged for creating and manipulating ASTs in compilers.

To gain hands-on experience, consider using Parser Generators such as Bison, ANTLR, or Yacc. These tools can draft a parser from a CFG and support AST construction. By creating a parser, CFG, and an AST for a simple language, you will gain a cement solid understanding of how an abstract syntax tree is built, manipulated, and used in a compiler.

ASTs and Parser Generators are truly fascinating and deeply central elements of compiler construction. Through their incredible capacity to break down and depict code structures, they unlock the extraordinary potential of programming and illuminate the productiveness of compiler operations. The voyage through ASTs and parsers demonstrates how intricate details conjure up an incredible system that has powered the software revolution. This enlightening journey amplifies our respect and awe for the riddles and rhythm of computer science.

# Chapter 10. Semantic Analysis: A Deeper Layer of Understanding

Since compilers were conceived, semantic analysis has played a critical role in ensuring that the meaning of computer programs is accurately represented and understood. As an invaluable phase in the compiler construction process, semantic analysis adds a deeper layer of understanding to the compilation process.

The journey of transforming a high-level programming language into machine readable code is remarkably intricate. Semantic analysis adds to this mystique by providing the critical function of validating syntax-defined constructs in relation to their meaning.

## 10.1. The Role of Semantic Analysis

We should first understand what semantic analysis is before diving into its comprehensive details and intricacies. Semantic analysis can be considered the bridge between syntax analysis and code generation. It verifies the semantic validity of the parse tree generated by the parser (part of the syntax analysis phase) to ensure that the program has meaning in the context of the programming language's rules.

One key responsibility of semantic analysis is checking for semantic errors in the source code. These errors typically arise from operations that are not semantically logical, such as adding an integer to a string, using a variable that has not been declared, violating scope rules, and other contradictory actions.

# 10.2. The Process of Semantic Analysis

There are many operations that occur during this phase, each contributing to the overall understanding and machine-level translation of the high-level source code. Here are the principal stages of semantic analysis:

1. **Type checking:** Here, the semantic analyzer verifies that operations are carried out on compatible types. If you attempt to add an integer and a string, a semantic error occurs, and the type checker sounds the alarm.

2. **Declarations:** Verification of whether a variable or a function has been declared before its usage is another critical job of semantic analysis.

3. **Scope resolution:** The semantic analyzer also verifies the scope rules of the programming languages and checks their correct application

This list of operations isn't exhaustive, but it does give a snapshot of the complex tasks involved in semantic analysis.

# 10.3. Data Structures in Semantic Analysis

Several significant data structures are used in semantic analysis, providing the architectural framework for this critical phase of compiler construction. One such vital structure is the Symbol Table.

Each identifier (such as a variable name) in the program is stored in the Symbol Table along with information about its declaration, type, scope, and other pertinent details. This table is used extensively in various semantic checking operations in order to verify whether an identifier is declared before use, to check type compatibility and more.

Moreover, while performing semantic analysis, an Annotated Syntax Tree or Annotated Parse Tree is used, which is an enhancement of the Abstract Syntax Tree constructed during the syntax analysis phase. The Annotated Parse Tree includes additional semantic information about each node, which makes it easier to perform the operations of semantic analysis.

## 10.4. Semantic Analysis: The Deeper Layer

Let's delve into the deeper layer of semantic analysis. As mentioned, semantic analysis serves to check the semantic constraints, and it generates useful information for the subsequent stage of the compiler, i.e., code generation.

Semantic errors are quite tricky to handle. A human can easily distinguish between the sentences, "I am reading a book" and "Book is reading me a I," but a machine without semantic rules might not. Both sentences, per syntax rules, can be valid, but semantically only the first one makes sense. And that's the beauty of semantic analysis. It understands beyond syntax structure and assesses coherent meaning.

Semantic routines, either attribute grammar or syntax-directed translation rules specified for each basis set, are executed to check the constraints.

## 10.5. Wrapping Up Semantic Analysis

To sum up, semantic analysis is a significant bridge between parse trees and actual code generation. Not only does it perform an inventory check on the syntax-defined constructs, but it also pours in meaning by quantifying the relationships between them.

The heavy reliance on data structures like symbol tables and annotated parse trees also underscores the overlap between different stages of compiler construction. Ultimately, the potency of semantic analysis lies in its ability to validate meaning - a crucial feat in compiling accurate and efficient machine language programs.

Indeed, compiler construction has its share of complex domains, and semantic analysis is one such territory. Yet, with a conceptual understanding of the task at hand and an appreciation for the techniques used, anyone can grasp the profundities of this often overlooked yet essential area in compiler design.

Semantic analysis not only broadens our understanding of compiler construction but also enriches our appreciation of how programming languages are transformed into a format that our machines can comprehend and execute. This unseen magic aids us every day as we code, debug, and build the algorithmic future.

Remember what semantic analysis does the next time you get a type compatibility error. It's not just an error message; it's a peek into the awe-inspiring world of compiler construction!

# Chapter 11. Optimization and Code Generation: The Final Steps

Before diving into the process of optimization and code generation, it is essential to understand the pivotal role they play in the world of compiler construction. A compiler's task doesn't cease at just parsing the source code and constructing the abstract syntax tree. It needs to march further and develop a magic wand that transforms the high-level language into low-level code or machine language. And this is where the bitter-sweet journey of optimization and code generation begins.

## 11.1. Understanding Optimization

Optimization in compiler construction lies in enhancing the efficiency of the resultant code. Solving the puzzle of optimization involves juggling between multiple criteria. These can be reducing the computation time or lessening the memory needed to execute the program, resulting in faster, better-performing software. Let's deep dive into the various phases of optimization.

### 11.1.1. High Level Optimization

This type of optimization occurs before or during the syntax analyzing phase. High-level optimizations encompass operations like code simplification, dead code removal, and loop optimization, which are performed using the source code's syntax tree.

1. **Code Simplification**: This strategy looks for reductions in computation. Consider an example, the calculation x = y * 1. Here, no matter the value of 'y', 'x' is always equal to 'y'. Hence, we can simplify this to x = y.

2. **Dead Code Elimination**: At times, developers may write code that has no impact on the program's overall outcome. Such pieces of code simply consume computational resources without contributing towards the result. Eliminating these segments is called dead code elimination.

3. **Loop Optimization**: Loops are significant performance bottlenecks. Loop optimization techniques like loop unrolling, loop fusion, and loop-invariant code motion aim to reduce the time taken by loop calculations.

## 11.1.2. Middle Level Optimization

In this section, the compiler implements techniques that are independent of high-level language but correlate closely with the machine code.

1. **Control Flow Analysis**: This analysis observes the various paths through which control can flow during program execution. The resulting structure is known as the Control Flow Graph (CFG).

2. **Data Flow Analysis**: Using the CFG, we analyze how data values "flow" through the program, which helps in identifying optimal spots for data transformations.

## 11.1.3. Low Level Optimization

Low-level optimizations occur after intermediate code has been converted into machine-like code i.e., Assembly Language. This domain deals with the specifics of the target machine, like register allocation, instruction scheduling, and branch prediction.

1. **Register Allocation**: Processor registers are optimized to reduce redundant loads/stores and excess register usage.

2. **Instruction Scheduling**: The sequence of instructions is rearranged to maintain the processor's pipeline filled at all times, thereby optimizing the execution speed.

# 11.2. Clasping onto Code Generation

Code Generation is the final phase of our compiler journey, where all the syntactic and semantic analysis, optimizations are transformed into machine-understandable code. Let's delve into the tools, strategies, and intricacies of code generation.

## 11.2.1. Selection of Instructions

A critical step in code generation is the selection of the right sequence of machine instructions that would result into the desired program operation. The code generator uses information from the syntax and semantic analysis phases to convert constructs into machine instructions.

## 11.2.2. Register Allocation and Assignment

The processed intermediate code contains variables, which need to be assigned to machine registers. Proper and efficient management of registers is critical, as using fewer registers can lead to faster computations, while using more registers can result in additional memory accesses which slow down execution.

## 11.2.3. Evaluation of Expressions

Expression evaluation is one of the most critical tasks in code generation. Evaluating expressions involves reading values from memory, performing the operation, and writing the result back. Expression trees are constructed for this purpose and the traversal of these trees significantly impacts the computational speed.

## 11.2.4. Instruction Scheduling

Within the CPU pipeline, each instruction takes a specific time to execute. Proper instruction scheduling ensures that the CPU's resources are utilized efficiently by reducing stalls in the CPU pipeline, thus accelerating program execution.

## 11.2.5. Function call & return Sequences

Generating code for invoking and returning from subroutines or functions requires careful management of the call stack, passing and retrieving of parameters, and the storage of return addresses.

# 11.3. The Conclusion Voyage

The journey into the complex maze of Compiler Construction doesn't end here. The effective creation of an authentic compiler requires a deep understanding of the various aspects we've explored, along with further concepts like Error Handling, Intermediate Code Generation, and Symbol Tables. The arena of optimization and final code generation is indeed a fantastic voyage. It exhibits how compilers ensure speed, efficiency, and accuracy - all simultaneously. It does demand keen interest and a meticulous approach. But remember, every major innovation was once a crazy idea explored with relentless curiosity. Happy Exploring!

# Chapter 12. Exploring Advanced Topics in Compiler Design

Let's dive deep into the intricate aspects of compiler design - a subject that is as fascinating as it is complex. Each layer we peel back will lead us to a deeper understanding of the underpinnings that enable our computer programs to function.

## 12.1. Dissecting Compiler Phases

The structure and phases of a compiler is a complex architecture, best viewed through the lens of a pipeline. Source code traverses these phases, transforming into an executable program. An advanced study of compilers is incomplete without understanding this process.

1. **Lexical Analysis**: The compiler starts by breaking down the program into small chunks, or tokens such as operators, identifiers, and keywords.

2. **Syntax Analysis**: Also known as parsing, this phase verifies the syntax of the code against a formal grammar defined for the language.

3. **Semantic Analysis**: This phase ensures that statements and expressions in the code are semantically sound. Do operands in expressions have the appropriate types? Are variables declared before being used?

4. **Intermediate Code Generation**: The compiler then converts high-level language statements into an intermediary language, a step towards making source-machine agnostic assembly code.

5. **Code Optimization**: This phase seeks to improve intermediate code without affecting the program's functionality, bringing

better efficiency and use of system resources.

6. **Code Generation**: Here, the compiler produces the target program - typically in the form of machine or assembly code.

7. **Symbol Table Management**: This aspect of compilers helps manage identifiers' scope, type information, and location at runtime.

# 12.2. Parsers and Parser Generation

Parsers handle the heavy lifting during the syntax-analysis phase. They validate the structure of the source code against formal language grammars, spotting syntax errors that would otherwise cause program execution to go awry.

There are two categories of parsers: top-down and bottom-up. The former starts with the root of the parse tree and works its way down, while the latter starts at the leaves and aggregates upwards. It must be noted that bottom-up parsing techniques are more general and can handle a larger set of grammars.

Parser generation, the process of automatically producing parsers from grammar specifications, helps in language development and compiler construction. Tools like ANTLR, Berkley YACC (Yet Another Compiler Compiler), and Bison simplify this process. These tools accept a language's formal grammar and churn out a parser that can read said language.

# 12.3. Diving Into Intermediate Code Generation

The intermediate code generation phase strikes a balance between the high-level source code and the low-level target code. As a byproduct, it facilitates portability - the same intermediate representation can be translated into different machine languages.

Intermediate code is usually represented in three ways: Syntax Tree, Postfix Notation, and Three-Address Code. Syntax Trees and Postfix Notation give high-level, rudimentary representations. On the other hand, Three-Address Code (or TAC) is more detailed, which makes it suitable for optimization and final code generation.

## 12.4. Code Optimization: The Performance Improvisation

Optimization is the art of improving code efficiency without altering its external behavior. The optimization phase aims to reduce resource requirements like CPU time and memory space, while improving execution speed.

Optimization techniques can be classified into two categories: Machine-Independent and Machine-Dependent optimization. The former works with the intermediate code, focusing on the high-level view of the code, while the latter deals with the target code, paying heed to the specific architecture of the intended machine.

## 12.5. Code Generation: The Final Transformation

Code generation is the process of transforming optimized intermediate code into target code—typically machine or assembly language. It involves aspects like instruction selection, register allocation, and instruction scheduling. The quality of code generated significantly influences the speed and efficiency of the final executable program.

## 12.6. Abstract Syntax Trees

Abstract Syntax Trees (AST) provide a high-level representation of the source code structure. Consider the expression `a = b * -c`. An AST represents this as a tree, where each node is a construct from the code. ASTs offer an efficient way of dealing with expressions and help in tasks like code optimization and analysis.

Compiler construction is an intricate process, unfolding through a series of complex phases. It involves several advanced studies such as parser generation, intermediate code generation, code optimization, and dealing with abstract syntax trees. Each component intertwines to create the magic that transforms high-level code into executables. By understanding the depths of compiler construction, we hope to have shed some light on the enigmatic process that brings computer programs to life.

Remember, this is just the tip of the iceberg. The field of compiler design is vast, ever-changing, and ripe for exploration. Your journey has just begun! Happy exploring.